The Jungle Book

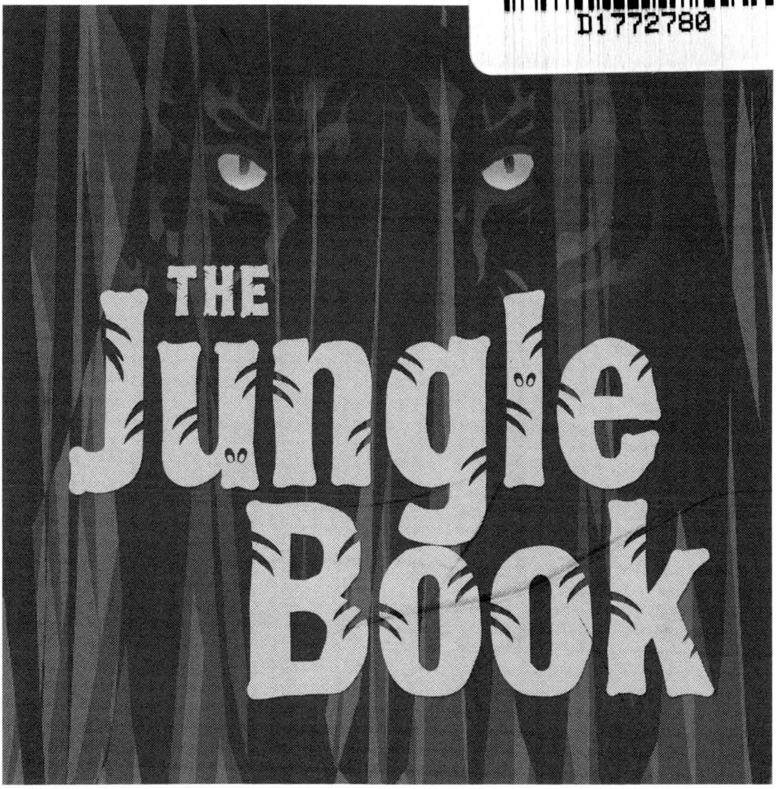

Written by
Briandaniel Oglesby

www.stagerights.com

THE JUNGLE BOOK
Copyright © 2014 by Briandaniel Oglesby
All Rights Reserved

All performances and public readings of THE JUNGLE BOOK are subject to royalties. It is fully protected under the copyright laws of the United States of America, of all countries covered by the International Copyright Union, of all countries covered by the Pan-American Copyright Convention and the Universal Copyright Convention, and all countries with which the United States has reciprocal copyright relations. All rights are strictly reserved.

No part of this book may be reproduced, stored in a retrieval system, or transmitted in any form, by any means, including mechanical, electronic, photocopying, recording, or otherwise, without the prior written permission of the author. Publication of this play does not necessarily imply that it is available for performance by amateurs or professionals. It is strongly recommended all interested parties apply to Steele Spring Stage Rights for performance rights before starting rehearsals or advertising.

No changes shall be made in the play for the purpose of your production without prior written consent. All billing stipulations in your license agreement must be strictly adhered to. No person, firm or entity may receive credit larger or more prominent than that accorded the Author.

For all stage performance inquiries, please contact:

Steele Spring Stage Rights
3845 Cazador Street
Los Angeles, CA 90065
(323) 739-0413
www.stagerights.com

ACKNOWLEDGMENTS

Big Idea Theatre in Sacramento, California, commissioned this adaptation for their 2014 Season. It opened November 7th. Benjamin Ismail was Artistic Director. The play was directed by Jouni Kirjola, assisted by Kara Ow. Alexa Slater was Stage Manager, assisted by Lizzy Poore. Puppets and masks were by Rachel Malin, set by Brian Watson, and props by Shaleen Schmutzer-Smith.

BALOO	Cameron Rose
BAGHEERA	Alexander Quiñonez
MOWGLI	Kane Young Chai
RAKSHA	Carrie Joyner
AKELA	Matthew Udall
SHERE KHAN	Ryan Snyder
KAA	Melissa Dixon
ALPHA and ENSEMBLE	Joseph Cady
BETA and ENSEMBLE	Maya-Nika Bewley
RALPH and DUKE and ENSEMBLE	Kevin Adamski
DEE-DEE and ENSEMBLE	Brianne Hidden-Wise
KITE and ENSEMBLE	Samantha Nakagaki

CHARACTER BREAKDOWN

BALOO: Baloo is a bear, a teacher of wolf cubs, and our narrator.

BAGHEERA: Bagheera is a panther, generally gruff and grumpy to everyone but Mowgli.

MOWGLI: Mowgli is the man's cub, raised by wolves. He struggles to fit in.

RAKSHA: Raksha is Mowgli's wolf mother. She's protective and strong.

AKELA: Akela is the head of the Seeonee wolf pack; the largest and oldest in the pack.

SHERE KHAN: Shere Khan is a man-eating tiger with his eyes on taking over the wolf pack.

KAA: Kaa is an aggressive boa constrictor happy to eat anyone who crosses his path; with his dance and eyes, he hypnotizes his prey.

ALPHA, BETA & RALPH: Alpha, Beta, and Ralph are young wolves of the Seeonee wolf pack. Alpha is their leader, and he doesn't much care for Mowgli. Ralph is a bit dopey.

DEE-DEE: Dee-Dee is a wealthy city-dwelling human; she aims to "civilize" Mowgli.

DUKE: Duke is Dee-Dee's husband, and you know he's oil money.

KITE: The "kite" is a vulture.

ENSEMBLE

WOLVES (OPTIONAL): Only Alpha, Beta, and Ralph have lines, but you can add a few more wolves to the pack.

MONKEYS: The Monkeys (or "Monkey People" or "Bandar-log") have a frenetic energy and don't like rules; one moment they crown Mowgli king, and the next they're throwing Mowgli into the snake pit.

SNAKES: The snakes (or "Poison People") live in this snake pit.

CITIZENS: The citizens have too much to do, with their work and cell phones and Starbucks.

KITES (OPTIONAL): Additional kites can take Ralph's skin in Chapter 5.

RECOMMENDED DOUBLING

RAKSHA > Ensemble (Monkeys, Citizens, Snakes)

AKELA > Ensemble (Monkeys, Citizens, Snakes)

SHERE-KHAN > Not doubled

KAA > **DEE-DEE** > Ensemble (Monkeys)

ALPHA > Ensemble (Monkeys, Citizens, Snakes)

BETA > **KITE** > Ensemble (Monkeys, Citizens, Snakes)

RALPH > **DUKE** > (Monkeys, Citizens, Snakes)

Doubling is possible, though not required. Although the gender pronouns in the script follow the corresponding characters in Kipling's *The Jungle Book*, these are flexible. When produced at Big Idea, Beta, Kite, and Kaa were all changed to female.

For KITE to be doubled with any of the wolves or Shere Khan, give the Kite's lines to Beta in Chapter 1.

SETTING

Chapter 1 and Chapter 2 take place in the jungle in an area ruled by the Seeonee wolf pack. Some indication of a ridge or rock should exist, as Shere Khan will later fall from this. Chapter 3 is in both the Lost City (ruins of an ancient civilization claimed by the monkeys) and in the jungle as Baloo and Bagheera track Mowgli down. Mowgli is thrust into a snake pit. Chapter 4 takes place in the city, which has some litter in it, and Dee-Dee's estate. Chapter 5 is once again in the jungle, but this one is full of garbage.

COSTUME SUGGESTIONS

This world is best realized through a mixture of puppets and masks. Below is a listing of how Big Idea Theatre realized these:

Masked Creatures:
- Panther (Bagheera)
- Bear (Baloo)
- The Tiger (Shere Khan)
- Monkeys (4+)

Puppet Creatures:
- Five Wolves (Alpha, Beta, Ralph, Raksha, and Akela)
- Kite
- Baby Mowgli
- Boa Constrictor (Kaa)

RUN TIME

75 Minutes without Intermission

(Intermission recommended)

PROLOGUE

We are in darkness— deep and inky— and in this darkness, the jungle grows like vines of sound. Let it quake. Let it roll over the audience. From this, BALOO emerges. Maybe he's conducting the jungle. He settles the sounds so he can introduce himself.

BALOO (NARRATOR): Hello, hi. I am Baloo, and I am a bear, but I am not a normal bear.

Normal bears are not narrators. Nor are they teachers. I am both. I am tasked with the edification of the wolf pack. I teach them jungle law and the stories of us Jungle People.

Listen to me, and you may stay alive.

    (Clears throat)

In a jungle, dark and deep,

Hunters hunt and creatures creep,

Betwixt vines and ferns, brush and leaves,

Hide yourself! You're not as safe as it seems,

Dangers crouch behind each tree,

Be wary for they will come for thee.

Listen, there! You hear that howl?

Akela's pack is on the prowl.

Always avoid the python's eyes,

A glance, a dance, and Kaa will hypnotize.

A tiger's roar should make you shiver,

For you may be Shere Khan's next dinner.

And when you fall, when you've lost the fight,

Your bones will be cleaned by the kite.

And should you find yourself today

The predator and not the prey,

Eat well, fill your stomach on fowl and beast,

Because tomorrow you may be the feast.

Hunger is a way of life, but there is another rule,

Followed only by the wolves, who are no fools—

BALOO (NARRATOR) [CONT'D]: The wolves they say, "You may be skin, you may be bone,

But learn you this: leave humankind alone."

CREATURES (*overlapping voices*): Just a bite a nibble a taste / one two maybe three / I am so hungry for human

BALOO: Leave them alone!

CREATURES: No good comes from humans.

> *BAGHEERA appears.*

BAGHEERA: Baloo, darlin'—

BALOO (NARRATOR): This is Bagheera, and he is a cat—

BAGHEERA: Panther, Baloo.

BALOO: Today's story— Riki-Tiki-Tavi!

BAGHEERA: No.

BALOO: Today's story— The White Seal.

BAGHEERA: No. It's time for Mowgli's Story.

BALOO: Are you sure? It has sad parts. And scary parts. And monkeys!

BOTH: Grr— Monkeys!

BALOO: And I say things that I regret. How about a story where I don't make humbling mistakes?

BAGHEERA: Baloo— it's time to tell Mowgli's story.

BALOO (NARRATOR): He always gets what he wants.

Today my duty is to share,

The story of Mowgli, a man's cub grown in my care.

BAGHEERA: Our care, you old sack.

BALOO (NARRATOR): And among the wolves in Akela's pack

Our hymnals open, take a look,

Verse one, we introduce, The Jungle Book.

CHAPTER 1
THE MAN'S CUB

As BALOO speaks, the WOLVES appear, and these wolves circle a few times, then settle into their respective wolf perches. We note a particular wolf, RAKSHA, and she is napping on a rock. She is sad. She is in mourning.

BALOO (NARRATOR): Chapter 1: The Man's Cub.

The Seeonee Wolf Pack, ruled by the great and honorable gray Akela, make their territory in the valley thick with jungle.

BETA *(to Ralph)*: You got the mouth of a jackal! And you got fleas. You caught them from a cat.

BALOO (NARRATOR): Tonight, the sky is empty except the stars, a dark night, good for hunting if you're a hunting creature. Tonight, several Seeonee wolves gather near a cave. One of them has heard a rumor.

RALPH: It's true. I swear.

BETA: Tales grow from your butt.

The WOLVES wrestle playfully.

ALPHA: Beta! Ralph! Is there a full moon, tonight? I swear, you'd think there's a full moon with all the howling in here.

BETA *(simultaneously)*: No.

RALPH *(simultaneously)*: I don't think so.

ALPHA: Have you become monkeys?

BETA *(simultaneously)*: No?

RALPH *(simultaneously)*: I'm still a wolf.

ALPHA: You're yapping like monkeys. Kaa will mistake you for monkeys with all that yapping, and rock pythons LOVE monkey meat.

WOLVES: We'll behave, Alpha. We're well-behaved, see!

They put themselves into submissive positions to show how well they'll behave. They end up fighting. ALPHA gets in on it.

ALPHA: Alright, that's it!

ALPHA pins RALPH.

Say uncle, say uncle!

RALPH: But you're my cousin!

BETA: I think we're bothering Auntie Raksha.

The WOLVES stop fooling around.

BALOO (NARRATOR): Our darlin' Raksha is deep in a jungle of her own, swallowed by a mournful darkness. She lost a cub to the thunder and lightning of a hunter's gun. This is the sad part.

RAKSHA: Go on and eat each other. At least, I'll be in peace.

RALPH: We're sorry, Auntie Raksha. It's just— the mountain tigers expelled Shere Khan! He's moved his territory to the valley.

BETA: Why would Shere Khan be here?

RALPH: Shere Khan's a man-eater. He eats mans.

BETA: Gross. That's against Jungle Law.

ALPHA: Ugh. There's no sport in humans. They are slow and soft and squishy, with teeth made to eat vegetables.

BETA: Humans taste of vomit and cholesterol.

BALOO (NARRATOR): That's a myth. The law, "Leave humans alone," isn't to protect man, and it isn't a culinary opinion— it's to protect the pack. Flesh costs flesh. If you eat a human, more humans come, and human hands hold rifles, muskets, shotguns, shovels that dig traps— they grow the red flower, which you—

BAGHEERA: Shhh, it's a theatre.

BALOO (NARRATOR) *(whispering)*: You know as "fire."

RALPH: Maybe he can stop 'em from taking over the valley!

RAKSHA: Ha! Nothing can stop them.

A noise.

RALPH: What's that?

BETA: It's a human.

RALPH: No it's not.

ALPHA: Shhh.

The WOLVES quiet.

We hear growling in the distance.

Something happens.

RALPH: You know, I'm actually happy that a man-eating tiger moved to the valley.

ALPHA: What part of "Shhh" don't you understand?

There's a sound. It's really close.

Ralph, go find out what that is.

RALPH: No! You do it.

BETA: He's afraid. He's shivering.

RALPH: I am not.

BETA: You're totally a fraidy cat.

RALPH: I am neither a cat nor afraid. Don't say such things.

The rustling in the bushes gets louder. RALPH approaches it.

Show yourself! I am wolf! I am a very scary predator!

The rustling grows even louder.

And I pounce.

Nothing.

It's nothing. *(Laughs)* I am so brave. Not like the other wolves, who startle at their own shadows.

THE JUNGLE BOOK

> *A BABY crawls from the bushes. It reaches and pets RALPH, who jumps up.*

RALPH (CONT'D): Help! Help! It's got me! I am caught! Help me! Oh, I am dead! *(Wait, it's a baby)* You can't scare me! I am scary! I am a predator. Growl. You are smaller than me.

BETA: What is it?

RALPH: It may be poisonous.

> *They circle the baby, nipping at it, sniffing it.*

WOLVES *(overlapping)*: It stinks / It's a man's cub / Do we eat it? Can we eat it? / The laws of the jungle / The laws apply to men, not to man's cubs. I say we eat it.

RAKSHA: Wolves— stand back.

> *RAKSHA approaches the man's cub. She sniffs it. Barks at it.*
>
> *The thing barks back.*
>
> *Is she going to eat it?*

It's so tiny. *(She doesn't, she sighs)* We return him to his parents.

WOLVES: His parents? / To the humans?

> *A ROAR! It rips through the stage. Everything trembles. We see the tiger's eyes. We may not see the tiger entirely, but he feels like he's everywhere.*

Shere Khan.

> *Another great roar.*

ALPHA: You talk to him, Ralph.

RALPH: You.

RAKSHA: What do you seek?

SHERE KHAN: Only what's mine!

BETA: He wants the cub.

RAKSHA: Who?

SHERE KHAN: The man! He belongs to me.

RAKSHA: He's a cub. He belongs to his human parents.

> *SHERE KHAN laughs.*

SHERE KHAN: You can return him to his parents, and they can tuck him in tonight. They can sing him a lullaby. Hurry before I finish digesting them.

BETA: Maybe we should?

RALPH: Yeah.

SHERE KHAN: He's my prey. Return him.

RAKSHA: Wolves don't take orders from clumsy cats who can't keep track of toddlers. Shere Khan, you let this little frog slip from your claws.

SHERE KHAN: Let me have his flesh, and I'll let you chew his bones, dogs.

WOLVES: Dogs!

RAKSHA: I have him. You don't. He is my prey by rights, to let live or kill if I please.

SHERE KHAN: Touch my food, lose your life. I'll rip you—

RAKSHA: SILENCE! I am Raksha the Demon! The man's cub, he shall live to run with the pack and hunt with the pack, and look you, hunter of little naked cubs, frog eater, he'll skip blithely through the forest wearing your skin on his back!

The other wolves don't know what to make of this.

ALPHA: Raksha?

SHERE KHAN: I'll swallow you whole and spit out your teeth—

RAKSHA: TRY! I am young and full of fight. I'll see your end before you see mine.

BALOO (NARRATOR): In a fair fight, Shere Khan could have run off any other wolf, save Akela the great gray. When Mother Wolf spoke, however, something told him he couldn't win. She would fight to the death.

SHERE KHAN: Female dog, bush-tailed thief, you are neither my quarrel nor my quarry—

Things might get real.

ALPHA: Shere Khan, Raksha, um, let's not spill blood tonight. The stars are out, so are the night creatures. We're wasting a good hunt. Let's bring this to the pack's council in a fortnight.

BALOO (NARRATOR): When the moon is full, the council meets on Seeonee Ridge, high above the tree-line.

BETA: Yeah, Akela can decide his fate.

ALPHA: To be sent off into the woods—

SHERE KHAN: For me!

ALPHA: Or for Raksha to keep him.

SHERE KHAN: No pack would foster a man cub... Shere Khan agrees.

ALPHA: Auntie Raksha? Akela's word is law.

RAKSHA: ...Fine.

RALPH: Oh, good.

RAKSHA: When the moon is up, we will see you, frog-eater.

SHERE KHAN: He'll be the end of you.

SHERE KHAN leaves.

RAKSHA: Alright, there, little one. You're mine now. At least until the moon is full.

BALOO (NARRATOR): The days pass quickly and soon the moon fills like a tick, bloating until round as an eyeball, and when it's whole and looking down on us, the pack council gathers.

RAKSHA: Baloo, Bagheera, watch the cub for me please.

BAGHEERA: I'm not sure—

RAKSHA: Watch him, please.

> *The BABY grabs his tail. BAGHEERA hisses.*
>
> *The BABY hisses right back.*
>
> *The BABY falls. The baby cries.*

BAGHEERA: It's making noise! Make it stop.

BALOO: You broke it?

BAGHEERA: I didn't. Make it stop.

Uh. Qui-et! Quiet.

> *BAGHEERA starts to sing a lullaby. Something like, "Rockabye, go to sleep or I'll kill you."*
>
> *The BABY quiets. The baby intrigues BAGHEERA.*

He's just a little frog, isn't he? Hello little frog.

> *A whistle, a howl. The council begins to gather. A KITE flies in.*
>
> *The WOLVES go through a ritual to open their council meeting. Perhaps this ritual involves howling. It certainly involves circling.*

WOLVES *(in unison)*: Born of water, rock, and mud

Deep inside runs ancient blood

Together we hunt, together we thrive

The council convenes to keep us alive!

ALPHA: Council is called to order!

Call forth Akela to preside!

WOLVES: AKELA AKELA AKELA!

> *AKELA enters. The PACK silences, bowing into submissive positions.*

AKELA: The birds are terrible gossips. Just the other day, a hummingbird buzzed in my ear. Tut tut, he said, a human has joined your pack. Nah, it can't be, this tiny bird is nothing but a whistling fart made to look like a jewel. But then a raven cawed out to me. Quoth the raven: AKELA RUNS WITH HUMANS! Should I believe what these little birds tell me? Surely no one in my pack would let a man walk with us.

RAKSHA: It's not a violation— it won't be. We'll make him one of us.

AKELA: Raksha. We've missed you at council.

Why do you want this thing? Humans killed—

RAKSHA: They did.

AKELA: And you want to raise it? This thing that will grow the red flower as soon as he can use his hands— that will curse us with "big bad wolf" the moment he can speak?

RAKSHA: We'll make him into a wolf, Akela. He'll chase the moon with us. He will be ours.

AKELA: If I grant you this, you become his parent, and parents are not allowed to speak on matters of their own children. They put the wants of their cubs above the needs of the pack. Will anyone else lend a voice to your cause…? Anyone?

BAGHEERA: I will speak!

WOLVES: YOU'RE NOT ALLOWED CAT!

AKELA: Sorry, Bagheera, you don't have speaking privileges. Anyone else?

BAGHEERA: Baloo, you're allowed to speak.

BALOO: It's not our business—

BAGHEERA: Baloo! Help her, please.

AKELA: Raksha, I'm sorry.

BAGHEERA: Baloo!

BALOO: You always get what you want.

Honorable Akela! I, Baloo, the bear and teacher, wish to speak.

AKELA: So granted, old friend.

BALOO: I teach your cubs the ways of the jungle, and I reckon I can teach the boy to be a wolf.

AKELA: You "reckon?"

BAGHEERA: Baloo.

BALOO: I promise! He'll never be a man with me around. He starts acting like a man, I'll put my teacherskills into him.

KITE: That won't work. That won't work.

He's a frog, a worm, a HUMAN.

A growl in the distance.

ALPHA: Shere Khan wants him. He's waiting in the forest.

AKELA: Let me see the frog.

AKELA examines the BABY. He growls. He snaps at it. The baby only laughs, copying Akela a bit.

AKELA (CONT'D): He's not afraid.

RAKSHA: He's named Mowgli.

This shocks AKELA.

AKELA: Raksha, Mowgli. After your—

RAKSHA: He'll be my son.

AKELA: Raksha, this man cub.

RAKSHA: Mowgli.

AKELA: This man cub is a risk. Boys become men, and men become hunters. Are you certain?

RAKSHA: I am here, aren't I?

AKELA: Alright... I am intrigued. This man cub seems to be helping you. He may be of use.

The boy will remain one of us until he grows old enough to fend for himself!

Growl in the distance. SHERE KHAN could hear that.

ALPHA: I OBJECT!

AKELA: At that point, if he is indeed a wolf, he may continue to run with the pack. *(For all the world to hear)* However let it be known, if he isn't one of us, he belongs to Shere Khan.

ALPHA & OTHER WOLVES: The tiger won't like that.

AKELA: Oh, that kitty cat. The cub is nothing more than a morsel now. When he's grown, he'll be a full meal, and to hunt a man will be a much more sporting proposition.

ALPHA: He won't be a wolf, Akela. You're delaying the inevitable.

AKELA: So say I, and Akela's word is law.

WOLVES: Akela's word is law!

KITE: That little frog, he's as good as eaten.

AKELA: Raksha— Mother Wolf, the boy is yours. Raise him well. Should he threaten our valley—

RAKSHA: I know.

AKELA: Good.

BALOO: Time to make little Mowgli into a wolf.

RAKSHA: Hello, little Mowgli. My Mowgli.

The BABY gurgles and laughs, and sounds a little like a wolf.

CHAPTER 2
HOW TO BE A WOLF

BALOO (NARRATOR): Chapter 2: How to Be a Wolf.

And so Mowgli grows up, raised in the Seeonee pack by Raksha, a doting wolf-mother.

> *MOWGLI appears. He's mid-sized. RAKSHA does something wolf-motherly to him. Maybe she licks him to get a spot out.*

MOWGLI: Mom. You don't gotta do that.

RAKSHA: Yes. I do.

MOWGLI: Mom!

RAKSHA: I'll be gone a few days.

MOWGLI: Why?

RAKSHA: The herd has migrated to the far side of the valley.

MOWGLI: Why?

RAKSHA: Never you mind. Just a few days, my little one. It'll be a good hunt. Bagheera and Baloo will take care of you.

MOWGLI: I like Bagheera. He's mean to everyone except me.

BALOO (NARRATOR): And what of Shere Khan you may ask?

> *RAKSHA exits.*

BAGHEERA: Shere Khan?

MOWGLI: Shere Khan!?

BAGHEERA *(narrating)*: Cats are patient creatures.

BALOO: They're jerks, that's what they are.

> *BAGHEERA sticks his tongue out.*

Cats can hold stock still at the edge of the waterhole for days, waiting for some slightly antisocial buffalo to get thirsty for the water that's over there, to wander and—

> *BAGHEERA cat-roars and pounces.*

BAGHEERA: RAR!

BALOO (NARRATOR): For this particular human, Shere Khan will wait years.

BAGHEERA *(narrating)*: Sometimes he stalks game at the edge of the valley, roaring from the cliffsides so that Mowgli knows that someday, someday he will face the man-eating tiger.

BALOO (NARRATOR): As for Mowgli

BAGHEERA *(narrating)*: He grows slowly.

BALOO (NARRATOR): He learns quickly!

> *MOWGLI attaches a vine to his butt.*

MOWGLI: This vine will be my tail.

BALOO (NARRATOR): The other wolves, his peers—

YOUNG WOLVES appear.

ALPHA: Look at the man.

MOWGLI: I'm a wolf! See— tail!

BALOO (NARRATOR): Young wolves are cruel. If they see a crack, they shove in their snouts and pry it open.

ALPHA: Can we eat him?

BETA: Pops says no. Jungle Law.

ALPHA: Jungle Blah. I want to eat him.

(To Mowgli)

Shere Khan will gobble you up.

BETA: He'll swallow you whole.

MOWGLI: Shere Khan doesn't scare me.

RALPH: I wonder what man cub tastes like.

MOWGLI: Not good!

RALPH licks him. He sputters and coughs.

RALPH: Not good at all!

MOWGLI: Told you!

ALPHA: Shere Khan doesn't think so.

BETA: One taste of human was all he needed.

ALPHA: One late night, he'll creep up behind you.

BETA: You won't hear him.

ALPHA: Your ears are human ears.

BETA: You won't see him.

ALPHA: Your eyes are human eyes.

And then—

RALPH: And then—

BETA: And then—

ALPHA: —He'll pounce!

ALPHA pounces on MOWGLI, but Mowgli pivots and grabs the wolf.

MOWGLI: He's a cat and I'm a wolf! Wolves chase cats!

ALPHA: Alright, let go of my ear.

MOWGLI: He's a cat! I'm a wolf!

ALPHA: Beta, Ralph, get this man cub off of me!

BAGHEERA *(narrating)*: This is when Baloo enters.

BALOO (OS): Rapscallion ankle-biters! Bushy-tailed flea-catchers! Class time!

> *WOLVES and MOWGLI scramble apart. BALOO enters, acting all teacher-like. The wolves mock him behind his back. [BAGHEERA exits the stage around now.]*

Line up! Hup to it!

ALPHA: Here he goes again.

BETA: Every morning.

BALOO: Listen to Baloo, for he is your teacher, and I am he, so listen to me. I am here to teacher you, I'll teacher you good— no, I shall teacher you well.

> *ALPHA copies him. The other WOLVES giggle. BALOO takes no notice.*

What wisdom I have sloshing around my noggin. You are shallow holes, and I am here to fill these holes with the water of my knowledge until it fills you up, and you can drink from it.

> *MOWGLI takes a turn mocking him. He copies his gesticulations perfectly.*

I bring light to darkness, and darkness to light! I write Jungle Law on your faces, jungle lore on your bodies, and jungle tales on your tails— Mowgli!

> *MOWGLI is caught.*

Don't you dare mock me, man cub! You're not an ape!

ALPHA: Not a wolf either.

MOWGLI: Shut up! I was just—

BALOO: Behave yourself, man cub. I know this stuff is easy for you, kiddo, but you gotta do it.

Class! How are we doing today, class?

WOLVES: We are bright-eyed and bushy-tailed, Baloo.

BALOO: Eager learners are living learners. It's particularly important these days when Kaa has been spotted in the jungle.

RALPH: KAA!

WOLVES *(overlapping)*: Where? / Where? / Let me see him! / Watch out for Kaa! / I'm ferocious! I'm not afraid of a python! / You're totally afraid! / No, I'm not.

BALOO: Stop that. Kaa is not here here. Pups, you needn't be scared. What do we say about Kaa?

YOUNG WOLVES AND MOWGLI: "Never look into his eyes, or else we'll meet with our demise."

BALOO: Once more, with feeling.

ALL: "NEVER LOOK INTO HIS EYES, OR ELSE WE'LL MEET WITH OUR DEMISE!"

BALOO: Why?

ALPHA: His eyes put a witchin' on you. Then he wraps himself around you, and squeezes 'til your eyeballs pop. Then he swallows you whole. Gulp, man cub.

BALOO: And Kaa is especially dangerous because he does not respond to what? The Master Words— correct! Review! What are the Master Words? Hello? Anyone? Beta! You.

> *BETA shrugs.*

Mowgli.

> *MOWGLI really doesn't like that he knows this.*

MOWGLI: The Master Words allow us to walk freely through the jungle. Inscribed in Jungle Law, pack predators use them to identify their cousins, according to the Treaty of the Eight Valley—

ALPHA: Blah blah blah.

BALOO: That's good, Mowgli. And what are these Master Words? Alpha.

ALPHA: I have sharp teeth and I can rip you apart?

BALOO: Incorrect! Wolfies, you need to listen like Mowgli listens. What if you find yourself face-to-face with the Poison People? A horde of wolf-eating boars? An angry bird? Mowgli— Master Words please!

MOWGLI: Why do you pick on me, Baloo?

BALOO: Mowgli.

MOWGLI: "We be of one blood, you and I"

WOLVES: Of course he would know.

BALOO: That's right! Now, everyone.

WOLVES & MOWGLI: "We be of one blood, you and I."

BALOO: Now! Say it in the language of the Poison People. You know? The serpents, the hooded snakes? What are the master words in cobra?

> *The WOLVES don't know. MOWGLI stays silent.*

You're embarrassing me. Mowgli, surely you remember.

MOWGLI: No I don't.

ALPHA: Yeah he does, he totally remembers.

BALOO: Mowgli.

> *MOWGLI shakes his head.*

Fine. Class! Repeat after me.

> *BALOO hisses. The class doesn't follow.*

You want me to get Bagheera??

WOLVES: Nooooo!

> *BALOO leads the CLASS in a snakey translation of "We be of one blood, you and I."*

BALOO: One more time:

> *The entire CLASS does it again. Maybe we even get the audience involved?*
>
> *ALPHA steals MOWGLI's tail.*

ALPHA: I got the human's tail.

> *That's it! MOWGLI explodes.*

MOWGLI: You're a dumb dog! I'll put a leash on you and make you beg for scraps!

ALPHA: Ha! Human!

MOWGLI: I'LL LIGHT YOUR TAIL ON FIRE!

> *The CLASS is hushed. Fire ruins everything.*

BALOO: Mowgli.

MOWGLI: What?

BALOO: Apologize.

MOWGLI: I'm sorry you're a dog.

BETA: You'll never be a wolf.

MOWGLI: I'll bite you right now!

BALOO: Hey hey hey! Stop that!

> *BALOO pries them apart.*

That's it, that's it! Class dismissed. Mowgli, you stay.

> *THE WOLVES celebrate the ending of the class.*

WOLVES: We should challenge authority every day!

> *They're gone. BALOO turns to the sulking MOWGLI.*

MOWGLI: They are mean to me. You are a mean old bear.

> *BALOO sucks at comforting MOWLGI.*

BALOO: Um. I'm sorry you feel that way. *(Uh, nope, not helping)* You're your own unique snowflake. *(Really not helping, aside)* I'm not good with the touchy-feely. This is when I make a big mistake: *(To Mowgli)* Buck up! Like an antelope buck! You don't see them down, unless we're eating them. Don't be a dead antelope, Mowgli.

MOWGLI: I wish you'da let Shere Khan eat me.

BALOO: Oh, oh, this is too much for me. I need Bagheera, he's good with the— yeah. Tell you what, how about you work on your howl, yeah, do your howl homework, and I'll get him?

THE JUNGLE BOOK

BALOO (CONT'D) *(narrating)*: This is when I leave.

> *BALOO leaves.*
>
> *MOWGLI is stuck for a moment. Then he starts working on his howl.*

MOWGLI: How.

How-ool

Hooow

> *There's a sound, copying the "Hoow."*

Whoa. How do you do?

> *We hear something like "How do you do?"*

Who's there?

> *Laughter, something that sounds like "Who's there."*

Show yourself.

> *A MONKEY appears.*

MONKEY: Show yourself.

MOWGLI: You look like me.

MONKEY: You look like me.

> *MOWGLI raises his hand.*
>
> *The MONKEY copies him.*
>
> *MOWGLI goes through a few more motions and the MONKEY copies him.*
>
> *Then the MONKEY leads.*
>
> *The MONKEY pounds his/her chest.*
>
> *MOWGLI pounds his chest.*

MONKEY: Don't copy me!

> *The MONKEY pushes MOWGLI down.*

I help you up.

> *MONKEY offers his/her hand to MOWGLI. Mowgli takes it.*

MONKEY: I throw you!

> *The MONKEY pulls MOWGLI too hard.*

MOWGLI: Ow!

MONKEY: Ow!

> *The MONKEY laughs. MOWGLI laughs along.*

MONKEY: Monkey people need a ruler-president-mayor-leader-king. You!

MOWGLI: Me?

MONKEY: You! Our king. Your own tribe. You'll hang in the trees, swing from vines. You'll throw rocks and dirt at mean bears.

BAGHEERA *(voice)*: Mooooow-gli!

MOWGLI: That's Uncle Bagheera.

The MONKEY laughs.

MOWGLI: He's a panther.

The MONKEY stops laughing and looks at him.

MONKEY: Bear's coming.

MOWGLI: No, not bear. Panther. He lives with a bear.

BAGHEERA *(voice)*: Where are you?

MOWGLI: Over here, Bagheera! Meet my friend!

The MONKEY leaves without MOWGLI seeing him.

BAGHEERA enters.

BAGHEERA: A friend?

MOWGLI: Where did he go?

We hear screeching in the distance, up a tree.

BAGHEERA: A monkey.

MOWGLI: He looked like me!

BAGHEERA: One of the monkey people. The Bandar-log.

MOWGLI: You never told me about the Monkey People, Bagheera.

MOWGLI climbs onto BAGHEERA.

BAGHEERA: Stay away from the Bandar-log, Mowgli.

MOWGLI: Why?

BAGHEERA: Monkeys don't obey the jungle laws.
The Bandar-log are cousins of humans— and jerks about it, too.

MOWGLI: The Monkey said I shall have a tribe all my own— and we'd throw rocks and dirt at old Baloo.

BAGHEERA: Mowgli, you're one of our pack.

MOWGLI: The wolves are mean to me. They want me to get eaten. I hate them.

BAGHEERA: You don't hate the pack.

MOWGLI: I do! I do. But the monkeys are nice. I know it.

BAGHEERA: The pups pick on you because their parents are angry at humans for chasing the herds to the far side of the valley.

MOWGLI: That's not me.

BAGHEERA: They pick on you because you're different.

MOWGLI: You're not a wolf neither.

BAGHEERA: That's right.

MOWGLI: You're a kitty cat!

BAGHEERA: Mowgli. Do you like to hurt animals? You are acting like a human.

MOWGLI: I am human. I'll never be a wolf.

BAGHEERA: Mowgli, touch my chin please.

MOWGLI: What? Why?

BAGHEERA: Go on.

MOWGLI: Weird.

BAGHEERA: Just do it.

MOWGLI: Fine. *(He does so)* Oh, what's that?

BAGHEERA: That's where the chain scarred me up.

MOWGLI: What chain? What is a chain?

BAGHEERA: Humans use chains to control animals.

> I was born in a circus. I played fetch for clowns. Clowns are kinds of humans. I was a pet cat, Mowgli. I lived in iron and concrete, alone, but I could smell the outside, a whiff from an open window, a smear of dirt on a trainer's shoe, and I knew, out there, darlin', out here, this is for me. It called to me. And one day, the call was so loud it drowned out my fear, and in a surge of strength, I snapped the chain, and I crashed through the gate into the unknown. I was deep in the jungle before I stopped running. But, once here, I didn't know what to do. No one had shown me. A clown is not a mother; a trainer is not a father. Where was the spidery man delivering me a can of brown cat-food? What are these things with fur, with feathers? Can't hunt, can't even speak to the others. I should go back, life in a cage is better than death in a jungle... That's when I met Baloo, who brought me to the Seeonee Pack. Baloo taught me to speak. He taught me to be a Jungle Person, and if I can become a Jungle Person, you can become a wolf.

MOWGLI: ...Okay.

BAGHEERA: Okay? You get what I'm saying?

MOWGLI: I think I do. Baloo!

BALOO reenters.

BALOO: What do you gotta say for yourself?

MOWGLI: I'm sorry, Baloo. You're trying to teacher me, I know.

BALOO: I am.

MOWGLI: I'm a buck for you. I buck up.

BALOO: Aww, there we go. You're a good boy.

BAGHEERA *(narrating)*: With Mowgli seemingly more at peace, they spend a relaxing day together.

BALOO: Now, why don't you help Baloo by clambering up one of these trees and grabbing some honey from that beehive?

BAGHEERA *(narrating)*: Mischief-making with bees, swimming in the creek, and late in the afternoon, when the sun stops to sit on its haunches and roast the valley, creatures in fur take naps.

BALOO: And so we do.

> *BALOO and BAGHEERA collapse asleep. MOWGLI pretends to go to sleep, but then gets up.*

MOWGLI *(to audience)*: Mowgli learned the lesson of the story: if you don't fit where you are, fit with someone else.

(To Monkey)

Hello? Monkey? Bandar-something?

I want to be King of the Monkeys. I want to play with you.

> *MOWGLI leaves, now in the arms of the BANDAR-LOG. He's spirited away.*
>
> *Screeching laughter. It is MOWGLI being carried from vine to vine to vine.*
>
> *BAGHEERA wakes up.*

BAGHEERA: What was that?

BALOO: Exit, pursued by me! Rararar.

> *BAGHEERA bangs on BALOO to get him awake.*

BAGHEERA: Get up, Baloo, something's wrong.

BALOO: Siesta time, Baggy-pants, time to sleep.

BAGREERA: Where's Mowgli?

BALOO: What's a Mowgli?

BAGHEERA: Mowgli is a missing!

> *BALOO wakes up.*

BALOO: Where's Mowgli? Mowgli is gone. Why didn't you wake me, Bagheera?

BAGHEERA: Stop playing games. MOOOOWGLI!!!

KITE: I— I— I—

BALOO: Great.

BAGHEERA: Vulture!

KITE: Kite, call me Kite.

BAGHEERA: Stop taunting us, Kite. We are not dying or dead.

KITE: Yet! Kites are patient. Your man cub is gone-gone.

BALOO: Not with you?

KITE: Not yet. Not yet.

THE JUNGLE BOOK

BAGHEERA: Dear Vul-Kite! Who is ever-so-helpful to the jungle, who returns us to the earth. Where is our man cub?

KITE: Monkey see, monkey take.

The boy you seek is with the apes.

BALOO: The apes! His mother will rip out our throats. Hello, Raksha the Demon, we lost your cub

BAGHEERA: Our friend.

BALOO: To the Monkey People, you see. But don't worry, he'll be their king— for a moment, then they'll tear him into pieces. Ooooh, Raksha will eat our faces and we'll deserve it.

BAGHEERA: Where are they!?

KITE motions.

KITE: There there there. Lost Lost Lost in the City! The Lost City.

BALOO: This is all my fault.

KITE: Beware, my friends earth-bound. 'Til we meet again— and we will meet again.

BAGHEERA: Come friend, let's go.

BALOO (NARRATOR): Chapter 3: A City, Lost and Forbidden. Note: this is one of the scary parts. Hold tight.

BALOO and BAGHEERA race off.

CHAPTER 3

A CITY, LOST AND FORBIDDEN

Now we're at the Lost City. A moment of stillness, maybe drumming from elsewhere. Then the MONKEY PEOPLE launch into an explosion of chaos. [Consider: "Monkey music" to indicate that we're in the space of the apes.]

They talk over each other, fight, bite, wrestle, and argue. One moment, they're hugging; the next, they're wrestling. One moment they're singing or chanting, the next they're yelling. [This can be both clowning and choreographed.]

The MONKEY that took MOWGLI enters. He/she whistles.

MONKEY: I brought something for us to play with.

A beat, then the MONKEYS return to chaos. They talk all over each other.

OTHER MONKEYS (*overlapping*): You brought a human / A mini man / What should we do? / Put him with the poison people / Is he tasty? / Chew his face off / We could! We could we could / Maybe he can show us the red flower / Yes, show us fire / Give him two sticks.

> *In the chaos, TWO MONKEYS bring on sticks. These monkeys start to fight with the sticks. Then all of the MONKEYS start to fight with the sticks.*

MOWGLI: What do I do?

MONKEYS: Whatever you want.

MOWGLI: Whatever I want?

MONKEYS: YEAH!

ORIGINAL MONKEY: WE NEED A LEADER!

MONKEYS: WE NEED A LEADER!

ORIGINAL MONKEY: A king, a leader, a president. Crown him King Mowgli!

MONKEYS: KING MOWGLI! KING MOWGLI! ALL HAIL KING MOWGLI!

> *An APE brings out a crown. They get distracted, putting the crown on their own heads.*

MOWGLI: Oh, okay then, alright.

> *The ORIGINAL MONKEY bulls over the others, grabbing the crown and screwing it on MOWGLI's head.*

MOWGLI: Oooo.

MONKEYS: Oooo.

> *The MONKEYS copy MOWGLI. After a bit of hesitation, Mowgli starts to party with the Monkeys.*
>
> *Monkey Music fades out, and we're once again with BAGHEERA and BALOO as they search for MOWGLI.*

BAGHEERA (*narrating*): MEANWHILE, Baloo and Bagheera stumble through the jungle—

BALOO: I think it's over here. Or maybe, maybe this way. Let's try this way.

BAGHEERA: Lost. They are lost.

BALOO: We're not lost. I know exactly where we are.

BAGHEERA: And where's that?

BALOO: The jungle.

BAGHEERA: This is no time for cleverness, Baloo.

BALOO: Fine, we're lost, and we're looking for the Lost City.

BAGHEERA: It's appropriately titled.

BALOO: Everything seems familiar. Those rocks— those woods, where I— but I don't remember those scaly rocks.

BAGHEERA: Rocks with scales?

Sssssss.

BALOO: Let's try this way.

BAGHEERA: I hear something. Hold still.

SSSSSSSS. The SNAKE is surrounding them.

KAA: Greetings friendsssss.

BAGHEERA: Kaa!

BALOO: Don't look at his eyes.

BALOO and BAGHEERA cover their eyes.

KAA: Think you'll turn to sssstone? I'm not that ugly, am I? Sssso rude.

BAGHEERA: Rude and breathing is better than the alternative.

KAA: No one wantssss to play with Kaa. This makesss Kaa ssssad. How about a hug?

BAGHEERA: No hugs!

KAA: My parentsss never hugged me. I have isssuesssssssss.

BALOO: We're sssorry to hear that, but we really have to ssssgo.

BAGHEERA: Wait. Kaa. Help us!

BALOO: What are you doing?

BAGHEERA: Monkeys are scared of Kaa.

BALOO: So am I, Bagheera.

BAGHEERA: Please sir, we are hunting the monkeys, the Bandar-log.

KAA: I despisssse them. They call me the mossst evil namesss.

BAGHEERA: I know. Uh. "Footless yellow earthworm."

BALOO: What are you doing?

BAGHEERA: Play along. Kaa can lead us to the Lost City. *(To Kaa)* They shouted it for all of the jungle to hear.

BALOO: "Footless, yellow earthworm"— without teeth! They said you can't eat anyone larger than a hornless goat's kid.

KAA: Tssssssss!

BALOO: That's a terrible insult.

BAGHEERA: Worst I ever did hear.

BALOO: And we're chasing after them.

KAA: And you sssssseeek my asssistance?

BALOO: Do you know where we can find the Lost City?

KAA: What wass losst I can find. But why oh why should I asssssist? When you so cruelly deny me my sssupper?

BALOO: He stole our man cub.

KAA: Aaaah, a man cub, hmmmmmmmman cub. A dining dissssspute.

BALOO: He's our responsibility.

> *BALOO stops covering his eyes.*

BAGHEERA: BALOO!

BALOO: Not our meal. We'd go to the ends of the earth for him. We'd look under every rock.

> *Pries up a rock.*

MOWGLI!

Unwrap every vine.

> *Looks under Kaa.*

MOWGLI!

KAA: Heeheehee— ticklessssss.

BALOO: You see, we, we love him.

KAA: Ahhhsssss... I know sssomething of love.

> *BAGHEERA uncovers his eyes, too, but is careful not to look at KAA.*

BAGHEERA: Help us, please.

The monkeys called you "toothless feckless cowardly yellow earthworm slithering on the ground."

KAA: I am suddenly hungry for ape tonight. Follow Kaa, pleassssse.

> *The SNAKE and BALOO and BAGHEERA exit.*
>
> *We're back at the Lost City. More chaos. One moment, they're acting like humans; the next, they're something else entirely. (Ex: a monkey pushes a stroller on, then two of the monkeys become the baby, then fight over being the baby.)*
>
> *MOWGLI at first seems to enjoy the party, but then he gets bounced around.*

MOWGLI: I'm hungry. I'm very very hungry. So, bring me food! Bring me food! I am your king.

MONKEYS: Food food, bring him food.

> *The MONKEYS race to bring him food. They bring it out, but then they start fighting over it, eating it, throwing it.*

MOWGLI: Hey! Hey! I am your king, give me the food.

MONKEYS: We have no kings. We have no rules. We are free!

MOWGLI: No rules, but I have a crown.

MONKEYS: Bah! Who cares?

> *MOWGLI climbs a tree and gets a banana (or something) of his own. A MONKEY takes it from him, destroys it or eats it.*

MOWGLI: No fair!

MONKEYS: "No fair!"

MOWGLI: I'm hungry!

MONKEYS: "I'm hungry!"

MOWGLI: Stupid monkeys. Stupid no-rule monkeys.

MONKEYS: We are great!

  We are wise!

  We are the most wonderful people in the jungle.

  We all say so, and so it must be true.

MOWGLI: Hello! I'm done. I want to leave now.

MONKEYS: When you're an ape, you're an ape all the way—

MONKEY: Until we tire of you.

MONKEYS: We're tired of kings! Coup d'etat! Coup d'etat! Coup d'etat!

> *The MONKEYS are turning on MOWGLI— then another MONKEY enters.*

ENTERING MONKEY: BEARS! BEARS! They come for the boy!

> *The MONKEYS shriek. They reveal a door with something that looks like a hooded snake on it.*

MONKEY *(to Mowgli)*: We're going to lock you with the Poison People.

MOWGLI: The Poison People? That sounds painful and deadly.

MONKEYS: POISON PEOPLE POISON PEOPLE POISON PEOPLE

MONKEY: Later we will play with thee if they let you live.

> *They toss him inside. And they laugh.*

MONKEYS: Prepare! THE BEARS ARE COMING!

> *The last of the MONKEYS vanish into their hiding spots.*
>
> *BALOO and BAGHEERA enter.*
>
> *The place is eerie quiet.*

BALOO: The Lost City.

BAGHEERA: It's quiet.

BALOO: What—

BAGHEERA: Shhh.

> *BALOO finds a piece of a doll.*

BALOO: Oh no!

BAGHEERA: What's wrong?

BALOO: It's Mowgli! They tore him apart! Alas, poor Mowgli, I knew him—

BAGHEERA: That's not him. Apes are full of— ow!

> *BAGHEERA is hit by a piece of fruit.*

BALOO: What's that— ow.

> *BALOO is hit by a piece of fruit.*

BAGHEERA: Oh, good, it's fruit. I thought it was— ow

> *More fruit hits them— the MONKEYS charge out.*

MONKEYS: BEARS!

BAGHEERA: I'm a panther!

MONKEYS: EAT THE BEARS!

BAGHEERA: Retreat!!!

> *THE MONKEYS chase BALOO and BAGHEERA off, howling all the way.*
>
> *We're suddenly in darkness. We're inside the cobra pit. It's very dark. Only a small shaft of light breaks through, revealing MOWGLI.*

MOWGLI: Hello? Hello.

> *COBRA: Ssssss.*
>
> *MOWGLI sees something… is it a face?*

Maybe you can help me out. *(It's a skeleton, nope)* You cannot help me. You are made of bones.

> *Laughter that sounds like sss-sss-sss-sss.*

Snakes. Lots of snakes.

> *Sssss. Sssss. Sssss.*

Are you friendly snakes? Are you garden snakes?

> *Ssss. Ssss. Ssss.*

SNAKES: We are the Poison People.

MOWGLI: Oh, how do I say, "We be of one blood you and I" in the language of the Poison People? The words have scattered like spooked rabbits—

Oooo-aahh?

No no no.

> *The SNAKES are getting closer.*

Twee-twee-twee.

NO!

> *The SNAKES rise up.*
>
> *MOWGLI gets it right, his eyes clenched tight.*

MOWGLI (CONT'D): Am I dead?

>*MOWGLI opens his eyes.*

SNAKES: Hoods down!
 Stand still little brother. You'll trample us.

MOWGLI: Standing still.

SNAKES: You know the Master Words. Thus, we ask— what do you need?

MOWGLI: The monkey people kidnapped me, only not because I wanted to go— because the wolves, I'm supposed to be a wolf, but they don't like me, and I'm wolf because a tiger ate my parents, and the monkeys are all "ahhh" and party and staying up past their bedtimes and they steal my food and all I want— I want to fit in. Can I be a snake?

SNAKES: No.

MOWGLI: Oh... Can you help me get out?

SNAKES: Out? / Out. He wants to get out. / I sssupossse. / Thissss way.

>*The SNAKES make the skeleton point the way out.*

>*[Meanwhile] BALOO and BAGHEERA are surrounded by the MONKEYS.*

BALOO: I think we got them.

BAGHEERA: You never think!

>*They have BALOO and BAGHEERA over a barrel. They drop a net on them.*

MONKEYS: Tonight we eat bears!

BALOO: Bagheera is not a bear.

BAGHEERA: Thank you, Baloo.

>*The MONKEYS scream and clap.*

MONKEYS: Eat the bears!

>*KAA's distinctive hiss. Uh oh.*

KAA: Hello, hello, hello.

MONKEYS: What is this?

KAA: I'm looking for a friend.

>*The MONKEYS' turn.*

>*They freeze as KAA does his dance. His eyes hypnotize.*

KAA: You'll be my friend?

MONKEY: We'll be your friend.

>*The MONKEYS move in unison together. Up and down.*

>*BALOO and BAGHEERA get out of the net.*

BALOO: Come on Baggy-pants. Bagheera?

But BAGHEERA is under KAA's spell, too.

Baggy?

BALOO falls under KAA's spell.

KAA: Look at all the friends I have.

MONKEYS, BALOO & BAGHEERA: We are all your friends.

KAA: I sssshall have you all for ssssupper.

MONKEYS, BALOO & BAGHEERA: You shall have us all for sssssuppper.

KAA: Move one ssstep closer to me.

They move one step closer.

Put your right paw in.

Put your right paw out.

Put your right paw in.

And ssstep closer to my mouth…

The MONKEYS, BALOO, and BAGHEERA all line up to be eaten by KAA.

I sssshalll sssstart with the big bear. A sssqueeze, and you ssssshall fit jussst right.

MOWGLI appears from the snake pit.

MOWGLI: Baloo, Bagheera! You're here. Take me home. I am not a monkey. Hello?

KAA: We've come to sssave you.

MOWGLI: Why won't they move?

KAA: I'll ssshow you.

MOWGLI turns around. He's looking into KAA's eyes.

MOWGLI: Are you Kaa?

KAA laughs.

KAA: I'll start with an appetizer made of man's cub, then a bit of bear, a plate of panther, and a mound of monkeys.

MOWGLI: I don't like that, Kaa.

KAA: I've never dined on man before. Today, I'll make an exception.

MOWGLI: Let them go. Please.

KAA: Go to sleep, little one.

It's not working.

MOWGLI: Let them go now.

KAA: I've got you in my sights.

Time to say goodnight.

You've looked into my eyes

Now you'll meet with your de—

> *MOWGLI isn't affected, so he bounds out of the python's coils, and grabs a sack or bucket and puts it over KAA'S head.*
>
> *The animals start to come out of the spell.*

Ssssssssoooo not funny! Take this off! Off! I WISH I HAD HANDS! I came to rescue you! I ssshould be rewarded with a meal— or ten.

> *The ANIMALS look at each other. They leave quickly.*

Let me out? Ooh, there's an echo. I hate my echo, it reminds me of my parents.

> *KAA slithers away.*

MOWGLI: Baloo! Bagheera!

> *MOWGLI hugs the animals.*

BAGHEERA: Oof. What? Oh. Mowgli.

MOWGLI: Baloo?

BAGHEERA: Ow. My head.

MOWGLI: What's wrong with him?

BALOO: You do the hokey-pokey—

BAGHEERA: Baloo? Baloo? BALOO!

BALOO: Good morning, Bagheera. What's for breakfast?

BAGHEERA:	**MOWGLI:**
Don't worry me like that.	It's not breakfast.

BALOO: I had the weirdest dream. Mowgli ran away and we got our tails handed to us by a horde of monkeys and almost eaten.

BAGHEERA: That wasn't a dream.

BALOO: Oh. So, I am in a lot of pain right now.

MOWGLI: I am sorry—

BAGHEERA: Let's go. Kaa may return.

> *They exit.*
>
> *We are in another part of the forest.*
>
> *We see a wolf enter. It is BETA, who is talking to himself and does not seem happy.*

BETA: "Beta, you stay behind while the big wolves go for a hunt."

What do you know?

> *We see a bit of the TIGER slide by— maybe a shadow. Maybe a tail.*

I am a great hunter. I'm ferocious. Grrr. Ferocious. Who's afraid of the Big Bad Wolf? The big bad—

> *A noise? A shadow?*

—wolf. The big bad—

> *A noise.*

—wolf?

SHERE KHAN'S VOICE: Tra-la-la-la la!

BETA: Who goes there? I am here with eighteen of my strongest friends! And they have rabies.

SHERE KHAN: You're alone, dear wolf. Alone.

BETA: Shere Khan.

SHERE KHAN: I got the eye of a tiger.

BETA: You're late.

SHERE KHAN: Dogs need more patience.

I bear a gift. Take a look.

> *BETA looks.*

BETA: A dead cow!

SHERE KHAN: All for you. So—

BETA: I love dead cow! Dead cow dead cow!

SHERE KHAN: Wolf?

BETA: Right! Look, the time isn't right. Yes, the man-cub embarrasses us, and we keep losing territory to the humans, and Akela forbids us from hunting them or cows, and some of the pack would side with you. But not enough. Akela's getting older, but he's not old.

SHERE KHAN: Tigers are patient creatures. The pack will belong to me.

BETA: Then we can eat so much cattle.

Thanks for the dead cow.

SHERE KHAN: Don't mention it. Really.

> *BETA and SHERE KHAN out.*
>
> *Back to BALOO and BAGHEERA, who stumble in a heap of pain.*

BALOO (NARRATOR): Freed from Kaa's hypnotic spell, Bagheera and Baloo return to the Seeonee Pack.

BAGHEERA: They begin to return.

BALOO (NARRATOR): It's a long trek, and Bagheera leads the way. The darkness of night ebbs away, and the obelisk of the morning sun is about to break over the valley walls.

MOWGLI: The Poison People obeyed me and Kaa's spell doesn't work on me! Kaa dances in foolish circles, but nothing happens to me. I'm a Master of Snakes. A Snake Master. Isn't that cool? Yeah, it's cool.

I need to pee.

MOWGLI exits.

BALOO: IT HURTS TO WALK!

BAGHEERA: Yes.

BALOO: And yet we walk walk walk.

Where are you taking us, Bagheera...?

BAGHEERA: My ears and sides are sore, and your neck and shoulders are bitten.

BALOO: Bagheera—

BAGHEERA: You were nearly eaten, Baloo. In front of me, while I watched.

BALOO: He learned his lesson. He won't wander away.

BAGHEERA: Did we learn our lesson? He's not safe with us.

MOWGLI can be seen— overhearing this conversation.

Some in the pack want him gone. They won't protect him. If he runs off again, he'll run directly into Shere Khan's maw, and the man-eating tiger may be less inclined to follow the old agreement.

BALOO: You've been here before.

BAGHEERA: Back when a chain made me bleed, I took this path— I can still smell my fear— and I found you.

BALOO: We're taking him to The City. We can't.

BAGHEERA: You're my world, Baloo. The pack is my world. It's not his. We've got to think of him.

And, if we can't make him a wolf, he belongs to Shere Khan.

BALOO: You may be right.

BAGHEERA: I am.

MOWGLI: You don't like me anymore?

Oh, no.

BALOO: Oh, no.

BAGHEERA: Mowgli, that's not it.

MOWGLI: You're hurt because of me. So you don't like me.

> We hear a song from out-of-sight. It's strange.

BALOO: Hide.

MOWGLI: What's that?

BALOO: Hide!

> BALOO and BAGHEERA hide.
>
> MOWGLI hides too, sort of.
>
> A WOMAN enters. She's human. A human woman. One of those. Uh oh.
>
> She is in modern dress. She's a little bit older the age of a mother. She's an early morning jogger.
>
> She doesn't see MOWGLI or the others.

JOGGING WOMAN: So many things to do today.

So many things to do.

So many things to do today.

So many things to do.

I've got so many things to do today

And I'm so darn late—

> She leaves. MOWGLI is intrigued. He's never seen a human before.

MOWGLI: She looks like me.

What language is she speaking?

Hello? Hello?

> He follows the WOMAN.
>
> BALOO and BAGHEERA hold each other. Lights begins to fade.

BALOO (NARRATOR): The tiger's tail we didn't forget.

Our story hasn't ended yet.

A respite now, a break for a minute or more.

We'll be right back with Chapter Four

INTERMISSION

CHAPTER 4
CITY LIFE

The CREATURES become CITIZENS who hustle and bustle in the city, weaving in and out of each other, suitcases and other articles of city life in hand.

CITIZENS: I'm late. I'm late!

Excuse me.

Excuse you!

Excuse yourself!

What's your excuse?

Hey, I'm walking here.

Hey, I'm walking here.

Hey, I'm walking here!

So many things to do today.

So many things to do.

I've got so many things to do today.

So many things to do.

Oooh, Starbucks!

> *All at once, all of the CITIZENS drink a cup of Starbucks coffee. In unison, they crush the cups and drop them.*

Phones don't text themselves

Farms don't farm themselves

Taxis don't drive themselves

Shelves don't stock themselves

> *MOWGLI is swept up in the hustling and bustling. He's overwhelmed.*

Beds don't make themselves. / So many things to do today.

Pesticides don't spray themselves. / So many things to do.

iPhones don't invent themselves. / So many things to today.

Chevys don't sell themselves. / So many things to do.

Ditches don't dig themselves. / So many things to do today. / Hey I'm walking here.

Trees don't paper themselves. / So many things to do. / Hey, I'm walking here.

Oil doesn't burn itself. / So many things to today. / Hey, I'm walking here.

War doesn't fight itself. / So many things to do. / Hey, I'm walking here.

CITIZENS ('D): Work! Doesn't do itself.

Work! Doesn't do itself.

> So many things So many things
>
> So many things So many things
>
>> Walking here walking here
>>
>> Walking here walking here

Drat! I'm late

Drat! I'm late

Work! Doesn't do itself. / So many things So many things / Walking here walking here / I'm late I'm late

Work! Doesn't do itself. / So many things So many things / Walking here walking here / I'm late I'm late

Work! Doesn't do itself. / So many things So many things / Walking here walking here / I'm late I'm late!

I'VE GOT SO MANY THINGS TO DO TODAY AND I'M SO DARN LATE!

MOWGLI: Rar-rar-rar?

CITIZENS are suddenly stopped by the presence of MOWGLI.

CITIZEN 1: It's a child.

CITIZEN 2: It's a creature.

CITIZEN 3: It's a homeless.

CITIZEN 4: It's a monster.

MOWGLI: Rar-rar-rar-oo-ahh-owl-rar-rar-rar-rah- rah! Ra-ooh-ra-ra-oo-raa-ra.

BALOO appears. He wears a "human" disguise, like a trenchcoat and flower hat.

BALOO (NARRATOR): Over here. It's Baloo. So, Mowgli is fluent in the languages of the jungle— he doesn't know a word of human. He has no way of telling them:

MOWGLI: Hi. I mean you no harm. I have left my pack. I'm tired and hungry. I would like to sleep somewhere that isn't rock and smelly.

BALOO (NARRATOR): All they can hear is:

MOWGLI: Rar rar aroo-oooeeeeee.

CITIZENS: Do you speak English? DO YOU SPEAK ENGLISH?

MOWGLI: Rar rar aroo?

CITIZENS: What were you, raised by wolves?

MOWGLI scratches himself. He's all wolf.

CITIZENS: Oh no!

CITIZEN 1: Oh yes!

CITIZENS: Raised by wolves?

MOWGLI: Rar rar rar.

CITIZENS: Big, Bad, Wolves.

MOWGLI: Arooo

CITIZENS (*overlapping*): Feral, ferocious, savage wolves. / He can't be near the children. / Wolves are dangers to society. / A wolf ate Little Red Riding Hood / Wolves killed the three little pigs / That wasn't real / Wolves ate all the sheep of the boy who cried wolf / Wolves have fleas / He's feral! / He's an immigrant! He'll take our jobs—

(In unison)

What should we do with him with him?

What should we do with him?

What should we do with him with him?

What should we do with him?

CITIZEN 1: We take him to a lab.

CITIZENS: Good idea! Good idea!

CITIZEN 2: Experiment on him! Like rats and monkeys!

CITIZENS: Good idea good idea / Like rats and monkeys!

CITIZEN 1: Psychological!

CITIZEN 2: Biological!

CITIZEN 3: Anthropological!

CITIZEN 4: Dermatalogical!

CITIZEN 3: Let's put him in a cage.

CITIZENS: I like that! I like that!

CITIZEN 4: Charge a fee— $5 to see.

CITIZENS: A fee! To see!

CITIZEN 3: Step right up, step right up, ladies and gentlemen, see the boy raised by wolves!

CITIZENS: Ooooh, I like that. I like that!

MOWGLI: Rar rar rar.

DEE-DEE THE WEALTHY WOMAN: Hands off him! He is not a circus freak, nor is he a lab rat. He's a piece of art. I will take him. I will civilize him. We can make him one of us. We can kill the wolf and save the boy.

CITIZENS: Kill the wolf and save the boy? Kill the wolf and save the boy!

DEE-DEE: He matches my décor. Much of what I own is jungle themed.

That's it, I've decided: he's mine. I have money, so you must do what I say.

CITIZENS: That's true / The Supreme Court said so.

> *The CITIZENS chant "Kill the wolf and save the boy" as they transform the stage into the wealthy woman's house.*

BALOO (NARRATOR): The one who annexed Mowgli is Dee-Dee the socialite.

DEE-DEE: Sheila Peters is going to DIE when she sees what I got. She bought an orphan from Ukraine, *Ukraine*, I have my very own wolf-boy.

BALOO (NARRATOR): She brings Mowgli into her household.

DEE-DEE: This is where you will be living, now. You're not to touch anything. What do I call you?

MOWGLI: Rar rar.

DEE-DEE: WHAT DO I CALL YOU?

MOWGLI: Mowgli.

DEE-DEE: Mowgli. Alright, Mowgli.

BALOO (NARRATOR): She plans to teacher him.

DEE-DEE: How to make a man— Lesson 1: Clothes make the man.

MOWGLI, THIS IS MY SERVANT. I THINK SHE HAS A NAME. SHE IS GOING TO WASH YOU!

> *A screen is put up, and behind it, they wash MOWGLI. We see his shadow as they wrestle with washing Mowgli. (OPTIONAL)*

DEE-DEE: My husband is Duke— DUKE! COME SEE WHAT I BOUGHT!— Duke builds houses and condos, he civilizes the jungle. I conquered him myself, you know. Took him over from his lonely bachelor ways, and if I can colonize a man like him, I certainly can CIVILIZE your ragged, rugged, alpine, lupine nature. DUKE??

> *MOWGLI emerges, now clean and in aggressively civilized clothing. Like a suit or something.*

MOWGLI: Rar rar rar.

BALOO (NARRATOR): Which means:

MOWGLI: THIS IS SO SCRATCHY WHY DO YOU PEOPLE DO THIS TO YOURSELF

> *MOWGLI scratches himself.*

DEE-DEE: We all must suffer for fashion. It's a magnificent sort of suffering. It separates us from the animals. And the poor.

MOWGLI: Rour.

> *BALOO: arm movement to indicate, "Which means"—*

You say things that sound stupid and I don't even speak your language!

DEE-DEE: You're going to have a fabulous, fabulous life.

MOWGLI: Rour.

BALOO (NARRATOR): So, Mowgli has found himself a new home and something like a family. Dee-Dee and Duke have the City in the palm of their hands— and unlike wolves, they have hands, and not paws— and with these hands they press buttons and use tools and shape the world. With these hands, they will shape Mowgli.

DEE-DEE: How to make a man— Lesson 6: Language! *(Holds up flashcards)* What is this?

A lawnmower.

MOWGLI: Lahwn-mower.

DEE-DEE: Correct. The help uses it to cut grass.

Grass must be of uniform height. What's this?

It's a car.

MOWGLI: A car. Traffic. Vroom.

DEE-DEE: Ugh! It is a Lincoln Towncar.

MOWGLI: Town-car.

BALOO (NARRATOR): Mowgli is bright. He speaks Wolf, Kite, Bear, Snake, Eagle, Pig, Pig Latin, Fish, Fish Latin, and soon, English.

DEE-DEE: And what is this?

A picture of a tiger.

MOWGLI: Shere Khan! Shere Khan!

MOWGLI gets up as if fighting Shere Khan. He's not afraid of him.

DEE-DEE: That is a tiger, darlin'.

MOWGLI: Shere Khan is a tiger.

BALOO (NARRATOR): Although Mowgli is quick to learn the language, humanity can be a lot harder to understand.

DEE-DEE: Lesson 44: The Value of Money.

MOWGLI: Money?

She pulls out a dollar.

Paper!

Why do we need money?

DEE-DEE: Food doesn't grow on trees.

MOWGLI: Yes it does.

DEE-DEE: Without jobs, people would be terribly idle. They would spend all day sleeping or making art.

BALOO (NARRATOR): A new language is one thing, but to make a man out of a wolf, he must master what the jungle people most fear.

Darkness.

DEE-DEE: Lesson 124—

DEE-DEE lights up a candle.

MOWGLI: The red flower.

DEE-DEE: Fire, Mowgli, fire.

Don't touch!

It's too late. OW!

MOWGLI: It bites!

Lights on.

DEE-DEE: Mowgli.

MOWLGI: It bites.

DEE-DEE: Sad. The wolves never let you play with fire. Touch here, not here.

MOWGLI: Let me try again.

BALOO (NARRATOR): Mowgli has so much to learn about what it means to be human, he's afraid he'll never catch up. Every step outside the house presents a new mystery.

They are outside. The CITIZENS are walking around. Maybe we hear "So many things to do today." A child plays. A poor person walks by.

DEE-DEE: Lesson 367: Class.

That man? He is poor. He is morally inferior.

MOWGLI: Oh.

The POOR MAN trips and falls. MOWGLI goes to help.

DEE-DEE: Go away! You filthy vagrant, how dare you touch my Mowgli.

MOWGLI: But he fell!

DEE-DEE: Some people are worthy of kindness, some are not.

MOWGLI: How can you tell?

DEE-DEE: By the clothes they wear and the cars they drive, silly.

MOWGLI: Rour.

DEE-DEE: Stop that. All this time and we haven't tamed the wild out of you, have we?

MOWGLI sees something. He starts to creep up on it.

BALOO (NARRATOR): You bet they haven't. I teachered him well.

MOWGLI: [Snake hiss meaning: We be of one blood you and I.]

A COBRA springs up suddenly, jumping into MOWGLI's hand. DEE-DEE shrieks. (So does the audience, we hope.)

MOWGLI: What's your name? You are so lost, my friend.

CITIZENS: He can talk with the animals?

CITIZEN 1: What a freak.

CITIZENS (*overlapping*): I don't like this at all. / Is he a witch? / I think he's a demon. / Animals aren't people / Animals are unclean / Next thing you know, he'll say they have souls / Animals are to be eaten / What's wrong with him / He's so strange / He tried to talk with my lobster dinner—

> (*In unison*)

The boy ain't right!

MOWGLI: I know what that means.

> *MOWGLI leaves carrying the SNAKE. The CITIZENS mumble-mumble as he goes.*

BALOO (NARRATOR): Mowgli heads to the edge of town with the snake.

> *MOWGLI sets the SNAKE free.*

MOWGLI: On the other side of this hill, there is a path that takes you to the jungle. This is where we part. Shere Khan awaits me beyond.

> *The SNAKE slithers away. MOWGLI notices:*

Where have all the trees gone?

> *We hear something in the trash.*

MOWGLI: Is someone there?

> *AKELA appears.*

AKELA: Just an old pup.

MOWGLI: Akela!

> *MOWGLI falls into a submissive position.*

AKELA: No need to bow. It's only a foolish dog, who recently trotted through a thicket of spiney, spikey flowers. Silly, silly Akela.

> *AKELA raises his paw. There's a thorn stuck into it.*

MOWGLI: A thorn.

AKELA: Young Akela would have gnawed off his paw. Youth, you know. But I am older now, and my paws have been very useful, don't you think?

> *MOWGLI takes AKELA's paw.*

MOWGLI: It's deep.

AKELA: You smell not you.

MOWGLI: It's called "soap."

AKELA: Ah, "soap." What strange fur you have.

MOWGLI: It's called, "Be careful. That's expensive."

AKELA: You are missed, you kn—

> *MOWGLI pulls it out.*

Ayaaaaooww!

MOWGLI: It's gone.

AKELA: Thank you.

MOWGLI: I was a thorn.

AKELA: What do you mean?

MOWGLI: I brought trouble to those I love. And pain. I didn't fit. And I wasn't an ape nor a snake either. I thought man's world would be better. Maybe they'd learn to love me.

AKELA: Have they? This world of noise and smell—

MOWGLI: I don't know. The noise is called traffic, and at least with the traffics, I don't hear Shere Khan roaring from the valley walls to remind me of my mortality.

AKELA: Before you, your mother had a cub named Mowgli, taken from the pack by a hunter's fire. There was a Mowgli-sized hole in our lives that she tried to fill with you. I'll be honest: when I learned you left, Mowgli, I was relieved. Your presence divided us. Without you, though... well, now there are two Mowgli-sized holes in our lives. You were not a thorn.

MOWGLI: You want me to return to the Seeonees?

AKELA: No.

MOWGLI: Oh.

AKELA: I lost the pack, Mowgli. It belongs to Shere Khan. Home always changes when you're gone.

MOWGLI: A tiger can't lead wolves.

AKELA: The pack hunts cattle now. And me, I hunt rats. I was expelled. Baloo and Bagheera, too.

MOWGLI: And my mother?

AKELA: Raksha, Mother Wolf, the Demon— she's still with the pack. And she doesn't hunt cattle.

MOWGLI: Good. What did Baloo and Bagheera tell her about me?

AKELA: That you love her. And that you're on an adventure.

MOWGLI: I am. I should be getting back.

AKELA: 'Til we meet again.

MOWGLI: Akela.

AKELA: Yes?

MOWGLI: We be of one blood, you and I.

AKELA gives him a nuzzle and lick.

AKELA: Blah.

MOWGLI: Soap.

We're once again inside DEE-DEE's house.

DUKE enters carrying something. DEE-DEE is on the phone.

DEE-DEE: I simply don't know what I am to do with him, Sheila. After all this time, he's still talking to the animals. And the poor. Just the other day, Darla's Pekingese—

DUKE: Dee-Dee! Hey! Give me attention.

DEE-DEE: I have to go. Duke is being needy. What do you need, Duke?

DUKE: My darlin'! Yo! I got a solution to your problem: Lesson whatever.

DEE-DEE: 841.

DUKE: Nothing inspires a man more than a taxidermied trophy. So gas up the ATV, set the traps, load the rifles— we got a man to make!

MOWGLI enters.

Mowgli! Come over here, take a look— Lesson 841: what an animal is good for. Boom!

He reveals— it's a wolf's skin.

MOWGLI: Mrs. Dee-Dee, Mr. Duke. *(He sees... oh my god! It's—)* Ralph! Ralph! Oh, my friend, my friend. Alas.

DUKE: It's going to make an awesome coat or throw pillow or something!

MOWGLI: You can't turn Ralph into a coat! This makes me so— argh.

MOWGLI growls in pain.

DUKE: You can't make friends with coats!

DEE-DEE: Mowgli, don't be so materialistic. It's only a coat.

DUKE: Tell you what— I'll take you for a hunt and you can bag one of these things for yourself. How's Saturday?

MOWGLI: I hate Saturdays! I need to leave. I need to go for a walk. I'm taking Ralph with me.

MOWGLI leaves, taking the skin with him.

DUKE: I think that went well, don't you?

CHAPTER 5
MOWGLI RETURNS

BALOO (NARRATOR): Chapter 5: Mowgli Returns.

BALOO (NARRATOR) (CONT'D): MOWGLI sprints out of the house, out of the city, off into the countryside, to the jungle. It is a journey he has not taken for some time. At first, he doesn't recognize it.

MOWGLI: The rocks look the same. That river looks... the color is not what it should be.

BALOO (NARRATOR): When I said he sprints out to the jungle, I mean he goes to where the jungle used to be.

MOWGLI: You can't lose a jungle like your keys or your marbles. Where did it go?

BALOO (NARRATOR): I told you there would be sad parts.

We hear the mooing of cows.

MOWGLI: Cows. Mooo. There is no jungle. There is only grass. And cows.

Mooooo.

Kite!

He caws: a KITE descends.

Hello, Kite. I have something for you:

Meaning RALPH.

MOWGLI: Take it. Return him to the earth.

KITE: [caw caw]

The KITE takes RALPH.

BALOO (NARRATOR): Mowgli closes his eyes. He imagines the vines, tree branches grasping at the sky like they want to peel the clouds apart. He remembers the—

Some of the sounds of the jungle.

A kind of music. He sits for hours.

MOWGLI: This used to be forest so lush you couldn't see as far as you could spit, with a canopy so thick, you couldn't tell if it was night or day. Now, the jungle is in the city, with the trees milled into walls of houses, ground with glue made of horse bone into Ikea furniture. Grassland feeds cows. The cattle doesn't speak to me. Cows don't speak jungle language or human talk. They don't speak. At all.

We hear something.

What's that? Show yourself! Are you friend? Are you foe? If you're Shere Khan—

BAGHEERA: I was friend.

MOWGLI: Bagheera!

BAGHEERA: Darlin', it's been so many moons. Look at you. What strange fur you've grown.

MOWGLI: Clothing. Itchy, scratchy clothing. *(He removes a piece of it)* Is Baloo here?

BAGHEERA: No. He has to narrate.

MOWGLI: Akela told me you were expelled from the pack.

> *Another piece gone.*

BAGHEERA: I was. Shere Khan wanted to repeal Jungle Law. I disagreed.

MOWGLI: What good is Jungle Law when there is no jungle? Maybe they should eat people. Maybe it will be good for the pack. Take the loggers. Cattle ranchers. Hunters.

BAGHEERA: And the hikers, naturalists, bird-watchers, hippies?

> *MOWGLI sighs.*

MOWGLI: You're right. Besides, eating humans will only lead to more trouble.

BAGHEERA: Now you sound like your mother.

Mowgli, I'm glad you still speak the languages of the jungle.

MOWGLI: I still dream in the languages of the jungle.

The city doesn't have a place for someone Mowgli-shaped. My body is human, and when that is gone, what is left will be shaped like the wolves.

BAGHEERA: I was wrong to bring you here.

> *MOWGLI makes a decision.*

MOWGLI: I'm going back to the pack.

BAGHEERA: Mowgli, Shere Khan will destroy you.

MOWGLI: He'll destroy them if I don't. He will, or the Dukes and Dee-Dees will.

Bagheera, I'm neither wolf nor man.

I am both.

And if I can't find a place in this world, I'll make another.

The council meets tonight. Go find Akela. I have something I need to get.

> *They exit.*

BALOO (NARRATOR): It's night in the valley. The moon is out and full. The council, or what's left of it, meets on Seeonee ridge, high above what used to be the tree-line.

> *The pack is ragged, beaten up from the years. One howls. The others join in.*
>
> *The opening ritual is the same, but beaten, tired, ending.*

WOLVES: Born of water, rock, and mud

Deep inside runs ancient blood

WOLVES (CONT'D): Together we hunt, together we thrive

The council convenes to keep us alive.

SHERE KHAN: Shere Khan! The baddest tiger in town takes his throne. And what a lovely throne it is.

First order of business: dealing with traitors.

And there is RAKSHA. She is oh-so-older.

RAKSHA: I suppose you mean me.

SHERE KHAN: Do you repent, dear Raksha? Are you a good dog or a bad dog?

RAKSHA: Bad for you.

SHERE KHAN: Goody goody! I was hoping you'd say something treasonous. The claws of Shere Khan's justice are sharp and swift. Thou art a most naughty, naughty dog. *(He is ready to make his decree, he waves his claws)* Dogs! There's your meal. Have at it. So says Shere Khan.

The WOLVES look at each other.

SHERE KHAN: Wolves! So says Shere Khan!

WOLVES: Uh. You want us to eat her? But she's—

SHERE KHAN: Flesh of a traitor is no different than the flesh of prey. Go on, chop chop.

Now! Or you'll be next.

RAKSHA: And who after that? And after that?

SHERE KHAN smells something.

SHERE KHAN: Wait a second.

SHERE KHAN sniffs again.

SHERE KHAN: The scent of fate.

Fee fie foe fub

I smell the blood of a man cub.

MOWGLI appears, in something closer to his old garb.

RAKSHA: Mowgli.

MOWGLI: Hi Mom!

RAKSHA: Look at you. My boy.

SHERE KHAN: Saving me a trip into town, are you? A cat can wait at the edge of a waterhole for ages for his quarry. And there you are. A feast. You'll go well with your mother.

MOWGLI: You were going to eat my mother?

> *BAGHEERA and AKELA appear. BALOO also enters the scene.*

SHERE KHAN: And look, he's brought more outcasts. The doddering dog, a bumbling bear and the panther with whom he has an inappropriate relationship.

We will dine well tonight, won't we pack?

No one but me gets a bite of the boy. Understand?

MOWGLI: Shere Khan. Am I still your foe?

SHERE KHAN: You always are. But I'm also your friend. Aside from your mother, I'm the only one who has always wanted you.

MOWGLI: Let me speak and take my mother, and we'll leave in peace.

SHERE KHAN: Except that she is not your real mother. I returned that one to the earth years ago.

MOWGLI: Shere Khan, you let me speak at this Council!

SHERE KHAN: I shiver.

MOWGLI: We be of one blood, you and I!

SHERE KHAN: We will be. Raaar!

> *MOWGLI brings out the fire.*

SHERE KHAN: You brought me the red flower.

MOWGLI: It grows in the city.

SHERE KHAN: You know, no one loved you.

MOWGLI: I don't care.

SHERE KHAN: I can say the word, and they'll dispatch you. One word. These dogs are mine.

MOWGLI: We be of one blood, you and I!

> *SHERE KHAN's whiskers are singed. He roars.*

SHERE KHAN: Wolves! Attack.

> *They don't.*

SHERE KHAN: Wolves! You cowards! Attack! It's only the red flower.

AKELA: Listen to Mowgli, wolves! By whatever respect you once had for me, please, listen!

SHERE KHAN: Beta! My loyal dog!

BETA: But I—

MOWGLI: I don't want to hurt you. You can come with me, to make a new pack. We'll leave the valley. We'll find a place without humans. We'll— AAARGH!

> *SHERE KHAN gets him good.*

> *MOWGLI turns and gives SHERE KHAN a nice singeing.*
>
> *SHERE KHAN roars and bats the fire out of his hand. It catches the river on fire.*

MOWGLI: Agh!

WOLVES: Shere Khan, the river is on fire.

> *SHERE KHAN and MOWGLI battle.*
>
> *[Does BETA bite SHERE KHAN?]*
>
> *SHERE KHAN charges one last time.*

ALPHA: Mowgli!

> *MOWGLI ducks.*
>
> *SHERE KHAN misses.*
>
> *He sails over them.*
>
> *He falls off Seeonee ridge.*
>
> *That's it for SHERE KHAN.*

MOWGLI: Where—

BAGHEERA: He's gone.

BALOO (NARRATOR): The fire on the river roars and thunders like a stampede of cattle. The pack retreats while the red stampede burns itself out. When it fades, they find him. Maybe it was the fall that ended him. Maybe it was the fear. Maybe he was too old, and it was his time. Regardless, that was the end of Shere Khan.

> *There's SHERE KHAN's body. It is broken.*

RAKSHA: You can wear his skin. I always said you would.

MOWGLI: No. Mother. I won't disgrace him. Kites!

> *MOWGLI calls the kites.*
>
> *The kites come and huddle around SHERE KHAN.*
>
> *They take him away: his body disappears.*
>
> *MOWGLI turns.*

The jungle of the valley is almost gone. The city has swallowed it. The lost city is no longer lost. Now it is the jungle that is lost. I am going into the mountains, where there's still jungle. There are lions and tigers up there— and soon there will be a Mowgli— and I hope there will be wolves. And panthers. And bears. We will start a new pack in the hills, a new family, of outcasts and misfits.

Come.

> *MOWGLI leaves. Some other members follow. Characters speak to audience:*

BALOO: And so Mowgli migrates up the hills, up the mountain, disappearing from prying humans to where there still is jungle. He starts his own pack of— well, it isn't just wolves.

BAGHEERA: Everyone is welcome. Each getting a vote in the council.

AKELA: Old Akela joins him— and he lives years longer than you thought he would, advising Mowgli along the way.

RAKSHA: His mother, who lives longer than she thought as well, loves the scent of the mountain air.

AKELA: The birds are different up here.

BALOO: Some of the old Seeonee wolves, too.

BAGHEERA: More of them than you would have expected.

BALOO: And of course,

BAGHEERA: Of course— Baloo, the teacher.

BALOO: And Bagheera, the panther.

BAGHEERA: Up in the mountains, Mowgli's pack thrives.

BALOO: Turns out, someone with the body of a man—

BAGHEERA: And the soul of a wolf

BALOO: can do a darn good job at leading a pack.

BAGHEERA: Hidden from humans.

BALOO: We teach Mountain Jungle Law to generation after generation. And we share the stories. This one, and others.

BAGHEERA: We tell it again and again.

BALOO: You may have heard it before. You may have heard this tale differently. It changes by generation. It bends to fit the time.

BAGHEERA: The core of the story remains the same. Each generation learns the Master Words by heart.

MOWGLI: We be of one blood, you and I.

> *The jungle begins to overtake the stage again.*

BALOO: In a mountain jungle, dark and deep,

Creatures thrive when creatures creep,

Betwixt vines and ferns, brush and leaves,

We hide ourselves. You're not as alone as it seems

Listen, there! You hear that howl?

Mowgli's pack is on the prowl.

BALOO (CONT'D): One rule gathers this pack
   We follow it, our family pact:

MOWGLI: "Far and wide you may roam,
   but when you're with the ones whom you love
   you are home"

BALOO: We hope some wisdom and fun from this you took—
   And so ends this tale from The Jungle Book.

END

PROPS

- Small Vine (Mowgli uses as a tail)
- Two Sticks
- Crown
- Food (fruit and the like for the monkey scene)
- Pieces of a doll
- Skeleton
- Net
- Sack or bucket
- The Dead Cow (can be offstage or hidden)
- Suitcases and articles of city life
- Coffee cups
- Trenchcoat and flower hat
- A screen (optional)
- Flashcards
- Dollar
- Candle / matches
- Cobra
- Trash
- Dee-Dee's phone
- Wolf skin (can be Ralph puppet)
- The "Red Flower" (fire on a stick)

Additional Titles From Stage Rights

Sasquatched! The Musical
Book, Music & Lyrics by Phil Darg

"The quirky new pop-rock musical that will keep your Bigfoot tappin'!" –*BroadwayWorld*

Sunscreen: check. Bug spray: check. Sasquatch... Sasquatch?!? Meet the misunderstood legend in this hilarious musical journey through the woods.

Musical | 4F, 7M, 1 Child, Ensemble | 1 hour 40 minutes

The Grimm World

by Adam Neubauer and Samantha Levenshus

"An all new high-octane storybook extravaganza!" –*BroadwayWorld*

Journey through a magical forest with Hansel & Gretel, Frog Prince, Cinderella, and others in this demented mash-up of the Brothers Grimm.

Family Comedy | 6F, 6M, Ensemble | 75 minutes

The Snow Queen

Book by Kirsten Brandt & Rick Lombardo | Music by Haddon Kime | Lyrics by Kirsten Brandt, Haddon Kime & Rick Lombardo | Additional Music by Rick Lombardo

"A fairy-tale that rocks!" –*The New York Times*

Urban steampunk and a pop-rock score amp up the Hans Christian Andersen classic that inspired the hit Disney movie *Frozen*.

Musical | 5F, 4M, Ensemble | 2 hours

Princess K.I.M.: The Musical
Created by Maryann Cocca-Leffler | Adapted by Maryann Cocca-Leffler & Toby Tarnow | Lyrics by Andrew Cass | Music by Andrew Cass & Premik Russell Tubbs

"Our community fell in love with Princess K.I.M.!" –*Monica Nadon, Director, TCT Community Players*

The popular children's books come to life onstage in this award-winning musical.

Musical | 11F, 5M, Ensemble | 110 Minutes

Additional Titles From Stage Rights

The Island of Dr. Moreau
Adapted for the stage by Mark Scharf

"Astonishing...Four Stars. This haunting tale of the thriller classic will have you enthralled by its sights, ensnared by its story, and excited to reach the dramatic conclusion." –*TheatreBloom*

The horrific creations of Dr. Moreau come to life on stage in H.G. Wells' haunting classic.

Drama | 7-11F, 4-6M Flexible | 2 hours

The Emporer's New Clothes
Book and Lyrics by Rob. Lauer
Music by Matt Bean

A smart new musical comedy that's always in fashion.

High fashion, pretentious celebrities and pompous politicians, abound as this famous Hans Christian Andersen tale is turned on its head.

Family Musical | 2F, 6M | 65 minutes

The Littlest Witch

Book by Tony Jerris
Music & Lyrics by Corinne Aquilina

"Funny and innocent enough for children, but enough adult humor for the whole family!" –*Brighton-Pittsford Post*

Every day is Halloween for this mischievous little wonder who causes mayhem wherever she goes.

Family Musical | 4F, 4M, Ensemble | 60 minutes

It's a Dog's Life

Book, Music & Lyrics by Peter Sham
Music by Randall Kramer
Additional Script Material by Steven D'Addieco

"A howling entertainment success!" –*The Buffalo Evening News*

With a street quality like a modern-day *Oliver*, this "tail" brings hope to a dog-eat-dog world.

Family Musical | 5F, 9M, Ensemble | 90 minutes

Made in the USA
San Bernardino, CA
26 October 2016